Sacred

100 Affirmations for Girls

Sacred

100 Affirmations for Girls

Mischa Green

Copyright © 2004 by Mischa Green

ISBN 0-9754191-3-7

All rights reserved. No part of this publication may be reproduced or transmitted in any form or by any means without written permission of this publisher.

Published by Morals & Value Press
2327 Harlem Avenue
Baltimore, Maryland 21216

Printed in the United States of America

Dedication

This book is dedicated to my mentee,
Zanada Moses.
My belief in you is so far reaching that I can already see the phenomenal woman you're going to be.

Introduction

It matters not what you have done. It matters not who you may have done it with. It matters not how you got involved in the first place, what matters is that you come to an understanding that you are not your behavior. What really, really matters is that you come to understand you are of value, and you have worth.

Because of the things I did with and to my body as a teenager. Because of the pain I caused my parents and my family. Because of the ugly things my family called me as a result of the pain I had caused them, I, at one point, thought there was no such thing as forgiveness. Others wouldn't forgive me. I couldn't forgive myself, and I did not believe that I was deserving of God's forgiveness either.

It took many, many years, two beautiful women, unconditional love from an amazing God, unceasing prayer, and a lot of determination, however, today, I am so in love with Mischa. I am proud of my accomplishments, and I look forward everyday to embracing all that I need to keep evolving into the wonderful woman God created me to be.

This is my earnest prayer for every young lady who experiences these affirmations. Read them until they become a part of who you are. Read them until the hurt doesn't hurt as much. Read them until you not only know better, but do better.

And if perhaps your difficulty is not having someone to believe in you, here's what I encourage you to do. Find a quiet place inside yourself—a place for you and no one else. Ask God to join you there, and tell Him you're in need of someone who cares; someone who can see beyond your past; someone who's love will grow and last. Return to this place as often as necessary, and before you know it you'll no longer have to worry about whether someone believes in you or cares, because God will have honored your plea and answered your prayer.

Sacred
Affirmations for Teen Girls

Sacred

☙

Feelings are a mirrored image of what's inside. They have a voice of their own that cannot be denied.

It's important to be honest about what you feel, because remember, what you fail to say your behavior will eventually reveal.

Sacred

☙

*My worth
is immeasurable.*

Sacred

☙

Every decision is important and needs to be thoroughly thought through.

Sacred

Being under the influence of too many voices can ill influence my personal choices.

Sacred

Loving myself is the first prerequisite for loving anyone else.

Sacred

☙

Everything God gave me—eyes, hair, lips, complexion—is what He purposed for me to have. I am fine just as I am.

Sacred

༶

Being a teenager is difficult enough without me adding grown up stuff to the process. I will learn to enjoy my adolescence.

Sacred

My body is a precious temple. Therefore, I will cherish and respect it as such.

Sacred

☙

When someone wrongs me it doesn't call for retaliation, it calls for a conversation.

Sacred

❦

Applauding myself is an investment in my internal wealth.

Sacred

I am a young lady . . . there is no ifs or maybes.

Sacred

☙

I call myself beautiful, and I mean every letter of it.

Sacred

My positive attitude will not be altered by someone else's bad mood.

Sacred

༂

There isn't a young man alive that I must have to survive.

Sacred

☙

I will not break under pressure. Rather, I will stand in the face of whatever.

Sacred

Being able to own my wrong symbolizes that I am mature and strong.

Sacred

*I will not pretend
just to have
someone call
me their friend.*

Sacred

༄

In me I believe.

Sacred

Surrounding myself with positivity can only produce the same.

Sacred

☙

Every new breath is an opportunity for me to make a fresh start.

Sacred

☙

Honesty is a wonderful quality that needs to be a central part of me.

Sacred

*Behind the lies
I continue to hide.
Hoping no one will see
what's really inside.*

*To live in truth
is my ultimate goal,
yet I keep giving the
lies so much control.*

Sacred

I love me dearly.

Sacred

I accept the invitation to live out my life's aspirations.

I'M A STAR

Sacred

Faith will get me through the toughest challenges and over the biggest hurdles.

Sacred

ൟ

*I am important,
my presence here
says so.*

Sacred

*Being different
is divine.*

Sacred

൨

I am a winner.

Sacred

I recognize my giftedness, and I celebrate my uniqueness.

Sacred

I must respect myself if I am to gain respect from anyone else.

Sacred

※

*Life is the joy
I make it.*

Sacred

☙

*I, not others,
determine who
I am, and who
I am to be.*

Sacred

At all cost, I must stay focused.

Sacred

☙

Winners win because they stay in the race. Losers lose because they allow distractions to compromise their pace.

Sacred

ଔ

Difficulties will come and difficulties will go. The question is — what did the difficullies teach me that I before didn't know.

Sacred

I am greatness waiting to take its rightful place.

Sacred

☙

I have potential.
I have ability.
I have a purpose.

Sacred

I will give real love, and I will be a recipient of the real love I give.

Sacred

༊

I will march to the beat of my own drum, for this is how my ancestors won.

Sacred

☙

Don't ask me why my standards are so high. I simply invite you to reach them—if you dare try.

Sacred

*Head up . . .
chest out . . .
this is what
I'm all about.*

Sacred

☙

*God grant me grace,
and grant me peace.
Grant me the ability
to believe in me.*

*Sometimes I get it,
and sometimes I don't,
but all the time I long to
be what You say I can —
not what the adversary
says I won't.*

Sacred

☙

I can change.

Sacred

I am letting go and moving on, because I absolutely refuse to stay stuck, broken, and torn.

Sacred

൪

Pursue truth and truth only.

Sacred

Remember, it never stays bad forever.

Sacred

☙

I have to come through in whatever I set out to do.

Sacred

☙

The meaner the world appears, the wiser I must become.

Sacred

I will not surrender to anything or anyone that fails to affirm my value.

Sacred

Anything that's able to stop me has been given my permission to do so.

Sacred

I go to school to learn, not to see how many heads I can turn.

Sacred

☙

*Stop—
think first.*

Sacred

I will not make excuses for myself. I will be accountable and ask, if necessary, for help.

Sacred

Success requires my best, especially when I feel like giving less.

Sacred

*I shall be healed
in every place that
hurt is revealed.*

Sacred

I don't have time to be consumed by everything that's on my mind.

Sacred

*Today is the day
I learn to stay out
of my own way.*

Sacred

☙

Drugs and alcohol are poisons my body can do without.

Sacred

☙

*To be for sale
is the ultimate
self betrayal.*

Sacred

☙

Doubt is not a stop on achievement's route.

Sacred

Empty places and lonely spaces are sometimes what we need before we are able to surrender and let God take the lead.

Because, it's sometimes the things we think we know that keep us from going the way God would have us go.

Sacred

Convincing myself is more important than convincing someone else.

Sacred

What's in my head matters more than what's on my back.

Sacred

❦

Talking issues through is the most effective way to distinguish what's false from what's true.

Sacred

In my heart will live love not hate; peace not violence; forgiveness not bitterness.

Sacred

൪

*Obedience
is essential.*

Sacred

Life can be a horrible nightmare, or a wonderful dream . . . it all boils down to what I want my existence to bring.

Sacred

☙

Discipline develops character.

Sacred

☙

I cannot and will not be distracted by things I cannot control.

Sacred

☙

A clear mind produces clear thoughts.

Sacred

☙

Education comes in many forms, I need to be knowledgeable about them all.

Sacred

ॐ

I am not a trash can, therefore I will not receive or carry garbage.

Sacred

☙

*Quitting
is not an option.*

Sacred

☙

Everybody has a place. That place, however, does not have to be in my space.

Sacred

*I forgive those who don't always know what to say.
And I forgive myself for the times I let their words get in my way.*

Sacred

☙

*I can,
therefore, I will.*

Sacred

☙

The manifestation of my greatest self has very little to do with an accumulation of financial wealth.

Sacred

༼༽

Reading welcomes new information that challenges my thinking and encourages my growth.

Sacred

※

I have control over the extent to which betrayal and disappointment will affect my forward motion.

Sacred

☙

*Abstinence is still the best assurance against sexually transmitted diseases and unwanted pregnancy—
this is truth,
not a mystery.*

Sacred

ೞ

*Looking in the mirror
the only thing I see
is all this beauty
looking back at me.*

*Instantly I smile
and say to myself—
"Girl, you got it going on
like nobody else."*

Sacred

*I cannot fail,
because a failure
I am not.*

Sacred

There is no such thing as enough when learning the right stuff.

Sacred

☙

God did not make a mistake when He allowed me to be.

Sacred

༃

Can't is the language spoken by cowards in fear. Can is the language I speak as courage lives here.

Sacred

I will not bow to the god of peer pressure.

Sacred

☙

*I grow based upon
my willingness to
embrace what
I don't know.*

Sacred

☙

May love and peace continually comfort me.

Sacred

ଓଃ

Growth is a lifelong process that I must choose to be a part of.

Sacred

Survivors make it despite the odds.

Sacred

☙

Saying no is not selfish — it's safe.

Sacred

ଓ

In order to get respect I must present myself respectful.

Sacred

❧

Belief in oneself is the first requirement for success.

Sacred

☙

God, help me to be thankful and appreciative for everything that You give.

Sacred

There are adults who know more than me. There are people who can see what I can't see. There are places I just can't be—and all of this is okay with me.

Sacred

Rules are not in place to violate my space as much as they are to keep me healthy and safe.

Sacred

My desire is to get the best out of life. To do this I must treat myself and other people right.

Sacred

Education and determination are authorization for elevation.

Sacred

*There are times
when I need to
do no more than
simply be still . . .
be quiet . . .
and listen to the
voice within.*

Sacred

○8

*Press on . . .
and on . . .
and on . . .
and on.*

Closing Words of Affirmation

In the event no one's told you today—I love you, I believe in you, and I am confident that you can and will become a woman of unparalleled greatness.

I admonish you to begin working toward fulfilling any dreams or aspirations you may have. Begin today learning how to nurture yourself by doing those things that bring you peace. Do not take your presence or your greatness for granted.

- Mischa

Ways To Nurture Yourself

1. Be honest with yourself. (If it doesn't feel right 9 times out of 10 it isn't right.)

2. Read inspiring books/magazine articles—and journal.

4. Go for "peace" walks to be with yourself.

5. Look in the mirror and say something affirming, truthful, and pleasant to yourself—everyday.

6. Take a nice long candle light bubble bath—once a week.

7. Believe and receive the positive about yourself. Hear and improve the negative about yourself.

Ordering Information

Name: __Nia__

Address: __926 Claymont Ave__

City, State, Zip: __Baltimore, MD, 21216__

__N/A__ Copies @ $10.00 = __N/A__

Please send check/money order in the amount of $10.00 plus $1.50 per book to:

    Morals & Values Press
    c/o Mischa Green
    2327 Harlem Avenue
    Baltimore, MD 21216

Visit us online at www.inlcdi.org

Nia
Townes

020807